IAN BOWRING
The Exploding Egg

With thanks to
GREG LAIDLER
for some of the ideas

Illustrations:
KIM GAMBLE

🏭 Angus&Robertson
An imprint of HarperCollins*Publishers*

EUREKA!

Over 2000 years ago a scientist named Archimedes ran naked and dripping through the streets of Syracuse shouting 'Eureka', which means 'I've found it'. What had led to this amazing sight?

Archimedes had made a scientific discovery in his bath. He had filled it full of water and got in, and the water had sloshed over the top and run all over the floor. So what, big deal, do it all the time, you say. But Archimedes was a scientist, and rather than just grumbling about having to mop up the mess, he noticed something. He realized that the volume of water *displaced* by him was equal to the volume of his body.

This is easy to see. Get one of your parents to cut you a block of wood 3″ x 3″ x 3″.

Its volume is 27 cubic inches. Fill a jar with water right to the top, put it in a larger container and gently force the block so it is just under the water level. Measure the volume of the water displaced into the larger container and you'll find that its volume is 27 cubic inches.

Archimedes used his discovery in a practical way to help the King of Syracuse. The king suspected the goldsmith who'd made his gold crown had cheated him by adding silver to the gold. Archimedes took pieces of pure silver and pure gold that were both the same weight as the crown. Silver is lighter than gold so the piece of silver was bigger than the piece of gold. Archimedes measured the volumes of the crown and the pieces of silver and gold by measuring the amounts of water they each displaced. He found that the volume of the crown was greater than the volume of the pure gold piece and less than the pure

silver piece. This meant that the crown was a mixture of gold and silver. The goldsmith had cheated the king for the last time!

Like Archimedes, you can do lots of experiments at home and learn some real science at the same time.

Blowing up an egg will

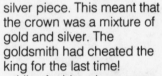

show you something about air pressure, making a simple color wheel will reveal something about the properties of light, and with just a cake pan, a sweater, a plastic bag and two rubber bands, you can learn something about electricity.

All the chemicals used in this book are ordinary household ones or are easy to obtain. Other items used are also often found at home or, if not, are not hard to get.

None of the activities are dangerous, though where hot water or sharp tools are required, ask an adult for help.

So, go forth and experiment! One day you too may be spotted running down the street shouting 'Eureka!'

Electric children

How well do you know your friends? Do they have powers beyond your imaginings? Let's find out.

You will need:

a cooperative friend wearing a woollen sweater

a wooden plank big enough to stand on, say 15" x 12"

4 dry blocks of soap or paraffin

a large plastic bag or raincoat

a small fluorescent light tube

a dark room

THE EXPERIMENT

Must be done in a dark room.

1

Stand the wooden board on the 4 cakes of soap or paraffin.

2

Get your friend, wearing the sweater, to stand on the board.

3

Rub your friend's back very briskly with the plastic bag or raincoat.

4

Give the fluorescent light tube to your friend to hold at one end, while you hold the other end.

What produces the light show?

By rubbing your friend's back, you create an electric charge. This charge travels through your friend's body, through his or her fingertips and into the fluorescent tube, causing it to light up.

3

The exploding egg

If eating boiled eggs isn't your favorite pastime, here's a startling way of disposing of them. And it's all in the name of science.

You will need:

a raw egg
a small saucepan
a glass bottle with a narrow neck (a milk bottle is okay)
a strip of paper approx. 1" x 5"
matches

THE EXPERIMENT

It would be a good idea to get an adult to help you with this experiment as you will need to use a stove and matches.

1
Boil the egg for ten minutes.

2
Let it cool then peel off the shell.

3
Twist the strip of paper.

4

4

Light the paper and drop it into the bottle.

5

Rest the egg on the top of the bottle, pointy end down.

6

Wait for the explosion. Clean up the mess!

What causes the egg to explode?

The burning paper heats the air in the bottle. This causes the air to expand and some of it escapes through the top of the bottle. As the air inside the bottle cools it contracts, leaving less air inside than before. The air pressure outside the bottle is now greater than that inside the bottle and the outside air tries to get in to balance the pressures. This forces the egg downwards, causing it to explode.

Pie pan generator

Get together with some of your friends and watch the sparks fly! The pie pan generator will give you a charge—positive and negative.

You will need:

a lightweight aluminum pie or cake pan
2 rubber bands
a plastic bag
a wool cloth

Note: This experiment works best on a dry, windy day.

THE EXPERIMENT

1
Stretch the two rubber bands across the pie pan at right angles to each other.

2
Lay the plastic bag on a table. Rub the bag briskly with the wool cloth then hold it up by one edge.

3

Lift the pan up by the rubber bands, keeping your fingers away from the metal, and hold it against the plastic bag.

4

Put the plastic bag down and touch the pan briefly with one of your fingers. What do you feel?

5

Now touch the pan to your ear. What do you hear? Do not let the pan get near your eyes, since sparks can damage them.

How does the generator work?

When you rub the bag with wool, the plastic receives a negative electric charge. Then, when you hold the pan near the bag and touch the metal, this negative charge on the plastic causes negative electricity in the metal to jump from the pan to your finger. This makes a spark. The pan is left with positive electricity. When you touch the pan to your ear, negative electricity jumps from you back to the metal, making a second spark.

Liquid lightness

When an oil tanker or an offshore oil well has a spill, the oil doesn't sink or mix with the water—it floats on the top. This happens because the oil is lighter than the water. This experiment shows that liquids have different weights.

You will need:

a tall, clear container with a lid (like a glass jar)

equal measures of water, glycerine (available from pharmacies) and cooking oil

a plastic Lego block (or something similar)

THE EXPERIMENT

1
Pour the glycerine, water and oil *gently* into the container.

2
Put lid on and tighten it.

3
Turn container upside down. What do you see?

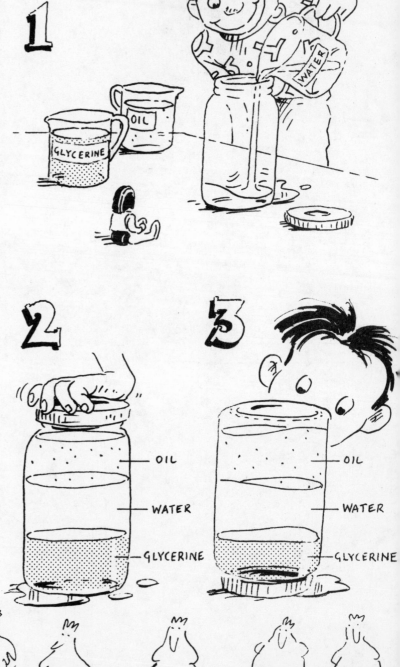

8

What has caused the different levels?

The same amount of different liquids will have a different weight. The lighter liquid will float on top of the heavier liquid.

Turn the bottle around and take off the lid. When the liquids have settled down, drop the Lego block into the liquid. What happens? Whether or not something floats in a liquid depends on its weight compared with the weight of the liquid. Heavier liquids can support objects that lighter liquids may not be able to.

Make your own hovercraft

Do you think it's possible to float on thin air? Here's the way to find out.

You will need:

a small, sturdy table (not one that your parents cherish), approximately 36" x 18"
20 balloons
a smooth floor
a piece of chalk
a friend

THE EXPERIMENT

1
Blow up the balloons, making sure they are all about the same size—about 6" in diameter.

2
Turn the table upside down on the floor. With the chalk trace an outline of the tabletop on the floor.

3
Place about half the balloons inside the marked area, spacing them evenly apart.

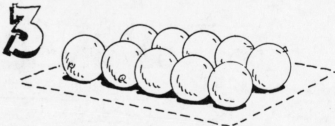

4

Turn the table upside down and place it gently on top of the balloons.

5

Push the rest of the balloons under the table, keeping them evenly spaced.

6

Ask your friend to steady the table on the balloons and then climb aboard. You are now supported by a cushion of air.

How does your craft hover?

Have you ever thought about what holds up cars? The tires, of course. But it's really the air inside the tires that supports the car. Hovercrafts work on the same principle— they ride on a cushion of air.

Water transport

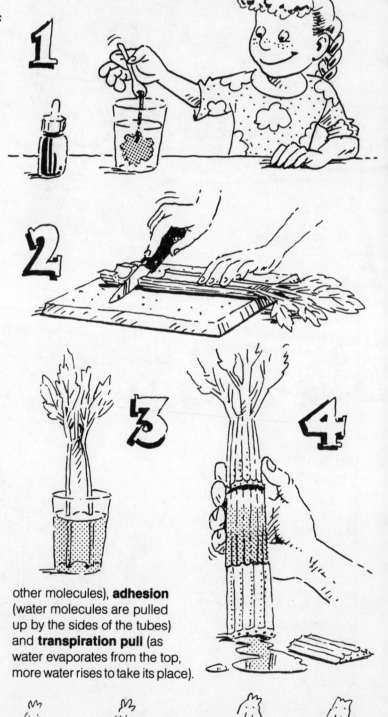

You probably know that plants absorb water through their roots. But have you ever wondered how the water gets to the rest of the plant?

You will need:

1 celery stalk
a knife
a small glass of water
a few drops of food dye

THE EXPERIMENT

1
Put the food dye into the water. (Use enough dye to brightly color the water.)

2
Cut about ½" off the bottom of the stalk of celery.

3
Put the celery in the glass of water, cut side down.

4
Leave the celery in the water for about half an hour. Use the knife to cut a section away from the outer skin of the celery stalk. What do you see?

How does the water travel up the celery?

There are tunnels in the celery which are called capillary tubes. The water travels through these tubes by three processes: **cohesion** (water molecules attract and pull up other molecules), **adhesion** (water molecules are pulled up by the sides of the tubes) and **transpiration pull** (as water evaporates from the top, more water rises to take its place).

Two-tone transport

Just as all roads don't lead to the same town, not all the water absorbed by a plant goes to the same place. This experiment will show you more about how water travels through plants.

You will need:

a white flower like a carnation or a gladiolus (try your local florist for flowers they're planning to throw out)
a sharp knife
2 glasses of water
2 different food dyes

THE EXPERIMENT

1
Put 1 teaspoon of dye into one glass of water and 1 teaspoon of the other dye into the other glass.

2
Cut about 5″ of the stalk of the flower in half from the bottom. (See Step 3—the flower has to be able to stand in 2 glasses.) Make sure you don't break the half stems or bend them too much. This could break the tubes in which the water travels.

3

Stand the glasses close together and put one part of the flower stalk in each glass. Make sure the stems don't touch the bottom of the glasses.

4

Leave the flower in the water overnight. What magic greets your eyes in the morning?

What produced your two tone flower?

The capillary tubes in the stalk of the flower lead to different parts of the flower. This means that some of the food coloring travels to one part of the flower, and the other coloring to another part.

Bottled rainbows

The food colorings and inks that you buy in shops are often made up of not one but many different colors. The science of revealing these different component colors is called paper chromatography.

You will need:

blotting paper, approx. 2" x 10"
a glass jar, 7–10" tall
an eye dropper
sticky tape
a pencil or a pen
4 food dyes of different colors

THE EXPERIMENT

1
Cut the blotting paper into 4 strips about ½" wide and the same length as the depth of the jar.

2
Tape one end of a strip of blotting paper to the pencil.

3
Using the eye dropper put a drop of food dye about 1" from the other end of the strip of blotting paper.

4
Pour water into the jar to a depth of approx. ¾".

5

Balance the pencil or pen on the top of the jar so that the blotting paper hangs down into the water. (The drop of dye must be above the water.)

6

Wait until the water soaks into the blotting paper and rises almost to the pencil. Remove and try another, repeating Steps 2 to 6 for each of your food dyes.

7

Look at the blotting paper. Can you see different colors at different heights on the blotting paper?

What put (or didn't put) the rainbow in your blotting paper

The water dissolves the drop of food coloring and this mixture is soaked up through the paper. The different chemicals in the mixture cling to the paper with different strengths. If one of the chemicals clings more strongly to the paper it will move up the paper more slowly. This is how the different chemicals become separated.

This process is used in scientific laboratories to identify small samples of substances and to check for purity.

Try the experiment with felt pens instead of food dyes (a brown pen is best because it is mixed from the greatest number of dyes). When you get to Step 3, draw a spot on the blotting paper about the same size as the drop of dye. Continue with the other steps.

Note: For this to work the ink must be water soluble. Some pens have spirit-based inks. If this is the case you will need to add some methylated spirits to the water.

Creating crystals

The dramatic crystal formations found in nature occur through evaporation. It is possible to create these fairyland structures (in miniature) in your own home.

You will need:

300 g crystal material (Epsom salts, copper sulphate, potash, alum or rock salt)
approx. 16 fl. oz. water
pipe cleaners
approx. 5″ cotton thread
a popsicle stick (a good excuse to buy an ice lolly—otherwise use a boring old pencil)
2 glass jars (each approx. 8 fl. oz., one with a neck at least 3″ in diameter)
a funnel
a coffee filter
a spoon

Note: You can get the crystal materials from most pharmacies (try health food shops for rock salt). Gardening shops sell copper sulphate as bluestone. If you use copper sulphate, remember it is **poisonous**. Keep it in a safe place away from small children and pets—and wash your hands after using it.

THE EXPERIMENT

1

Heat the water until it's almost boiling and pour it very carefully into the jar with the narrower neck. **(Ask an adult for help with this.)**

2

Add your crystal material slowly, stirring until it dissolves. Keep adding crystal material until you can't get any more to dissolve. This is called a **saturated** solution.

3

Place the coffee filter in the funnel and pour the mixture through the filter into the wide-necked jar. Make sure all the liquid goes through the filter. Let the solution cool to lukewarm.

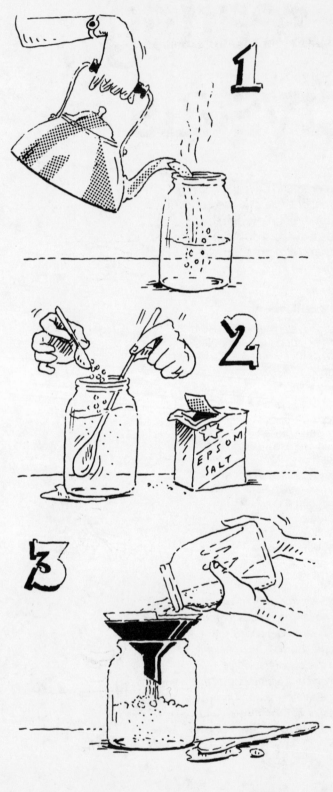

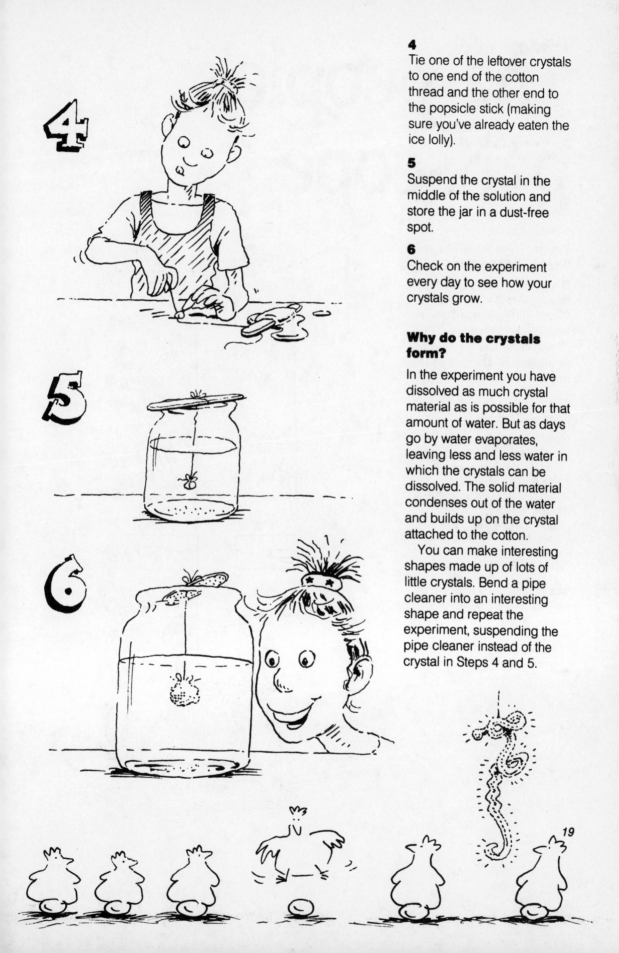

4
Tie one of the leftover crystals to one end of the cotton thread and the other end to the popsicle stick (making sure you've already eaten the ice lolly).

5
Suspend the crystal in the middle of the solution and store the jar in a dust-free spot.

6
Check on the experiment every day to see how your crystals grow.

Why do the crystals form?

In the experiment you have dissolved as much crystal material as is possible for that amount of water. But as days go by water evaporates, leaving less and less water in which the crystals can be dissolved. The solid material condenses out of the water and builds up on the crystal attached to the cotton.

You can make interesting shapes made up of lots of little crystals. Bend a pipe cleaner into an interesting shape and repeat the experiment, suspending the pipe cleaner instead of the crystal in Steps 4 and 5.

The people's periscope

It's not only naval engineers who can build periscopes—you can too. This activity is a little harder than some of the others and you will need to get an adult to help you, but it's worth the effort—your periscope will provide you with hours of fun.

You will need:

1 piece plywood, at least 22½" x 13½"

2 pieces of wood, each 25" x 2½" x 1" (this can be pressed wood or any timber offcut)

2 mirrors, each 3¾" x 2½" (these can be obtained from hardware shops or some department stores, or you could go to a glazier for offcuts—**see very important note on page 23**)

24 small nails

a saw

a hammer

a ruler

wood glue

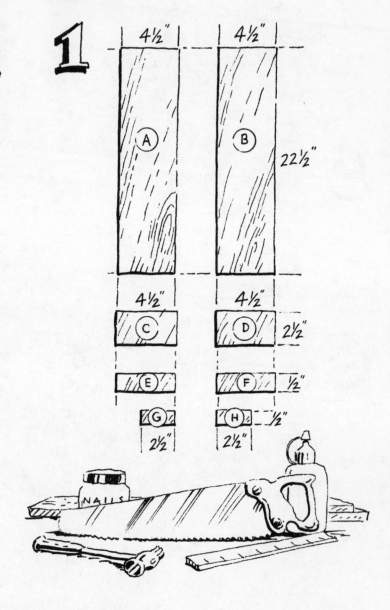

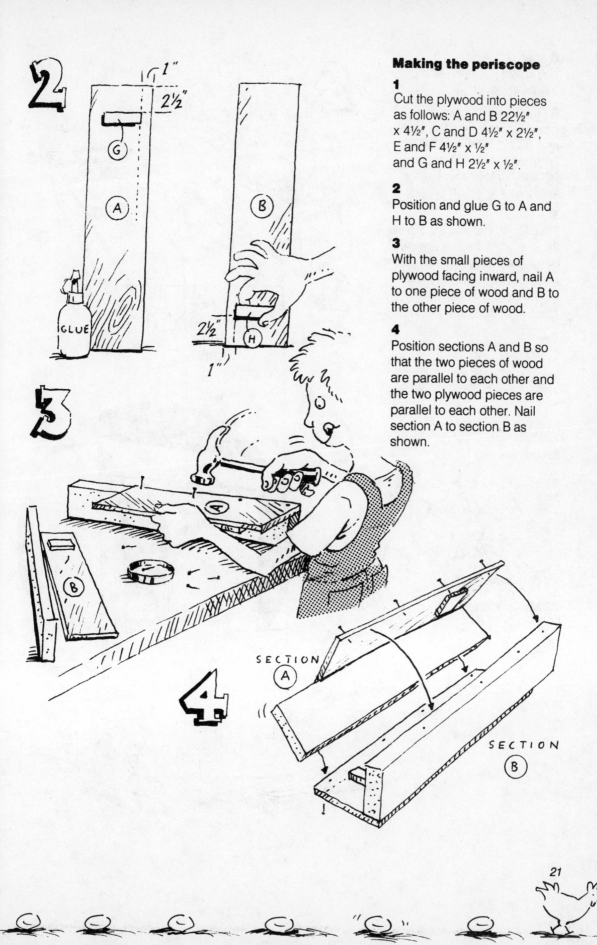

Making the periscope

1

Cut the plywood into pieces as follows: A and B 22½" x 4½", C and D 4½" x 2½", E and F 4½" x ½" and G and H 2½" x ½".

2

Position and glue G to A and H to B as shown.

3

With the small pieces of plywood facing inward, nail A to one piece of wood and B to the other piece of wood.

4

Position sections A and B so that the two pieces of wood are parallel to each other and the two plywood pieces are parallel to each other. Nail section A to section B as shown.

5

Nail E and F to each end of box as shown.

6

Fit one mirror at the top, shiny side facing outward, to sit between the wedge at the back and the one across the front that you've just put on.

7

Take C and nail it to the top of the box. Turn the box upside down and repeat Step 6. Nail D in position at this end. Your periscope is complete.

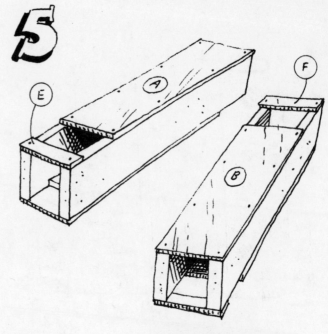

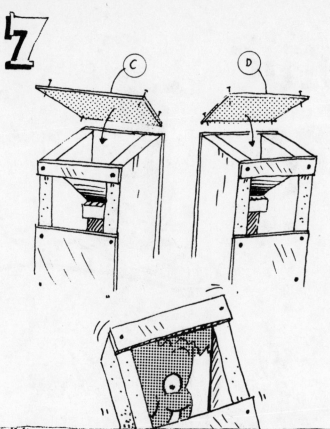

How does the periscope work?

The angle of the mirrors is the secret. Rays of light are reflected from a mirror at the same angle at which the light hits the mirror. We have designed our periscope so light comes in at one end, hits one mirror, goes straight up the middle of the periscope to the second mirror which reflects the light out and into your eye.

When your friends ask how it works, tell them that the angle of incidence equals the angle of reflection—that should impress 'em.

Very Important Note!

For your periscope to work it is essential that the mirrors are angled at 45° to the top and back of the box. If you can't get mirrors that are 3¾" long, you'll have to change the dimensions of the wood so that the mirrors are still at the correct angle. The position of the two plywood pieces used in Step 2 will also have to change.

Here is the formula to use to give you the width of the pieces of wood and the distance of the plywood pieces from the top and bottom of the box:

$$\sqrt{x^2 \div 2}$$

(x being the length of the mirror)

So if, for example, your mirrors are 4¼" long, you multiply 4¼" x 4¼", divide it by 2, then find the square root of that number; in this case, 9. Your pieces of wood will have to be 9" wide and the plywood wedges will have to be 9" from the top and bottom of the box.

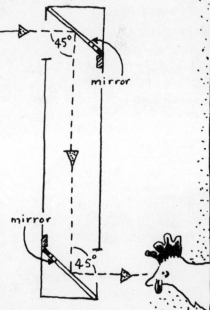

Electronic wizardry

In this experiment you learn to build a simple electrical circuit. We will use the circuit to find whether or not electricity passes through certain materials.

You will probably need to buy some of the parts for this experiment. Lamps, lamp sockets, battery holders, wire leads and alligator clips can be obtained quite cheaply from electronics stores.

You will need:

2 AA batteries
a battery holder
a lamp (2.5 volts, 0.3 amps)
a lamp socket
3 wire leads with alligator clips attached
materials and things to test such as a nail, a pencil, glass, a plastic container, a rubber band, a coin, wood, a stainless steel saucepan, a spoon, paper, matchstick

THE EXPERIMENT

1
Put the batteries in the battery holder.

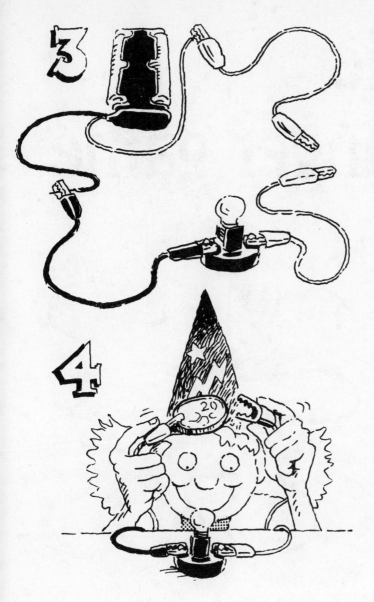

2
Screw the lamp into the lamp socket.

3
With the alligator clips attach wires to the lamp socket and battery holder as shown.

4
Take one of the items you have chosen to test and attach it to the two remaining alligator clips as shown. What happens? Does the lamp come on? Test the other items you have chosen.

Why does the lamp operate some times and not others?

Electricity can only pass along a circuit if it can flow through *everything* in that circuit. Some materials won't let electricity flow through them. If you have something in the circuit like this, electricity can't pass through the whole circuit so no electricity reaches the lamp.

If something lets electricity flow through it, it is called an electrical **conductor**. Materials which do not conduct electricity are called electrical **insulators**.

Warning!
Use batteries only for your source of electricity. Never experiment with electricity from power points – it is dangerous!

Electric coathanger game

This game tests just how steady your hand is. You can have lots of fun with a coathanger, a paperclip and the circuit you built on page 24.

You will need:

a steel or wire coathanger (like the ones that come from dry-cleaners)

a large paperclip (or a piece of stiff wire)

3 wire leads with alligator clips attached

a battery holder

2 AA batteries

a lamp or buzzer (a buzzer is probably more fun here)

THE EXPERIMENT

1

Set up a circuit as described on page 24, Steps 1 to 3, substituting a buzzer for the lamp if you want to.

2

Bend the coathanger into a shape similar to the one shown. The circular base must be big enough for the coathanger shape to stand up.

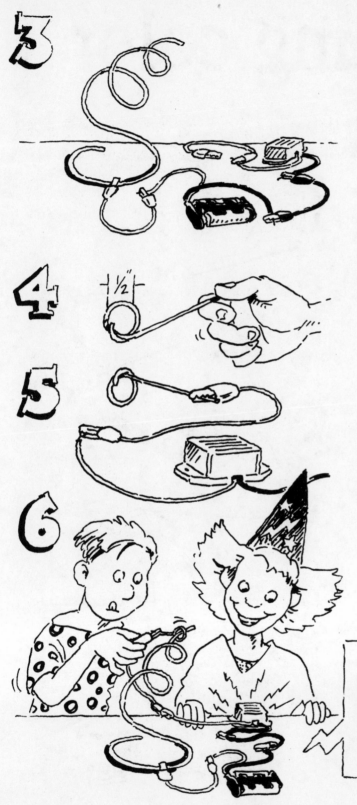

3

Using the alligator clips, connect the wire from the battery holder to the coathanger base loop.

4

Straighten the paperclip and then twist it into the shape shown. The loop should be about ½″ in diameter.

5

With the alligator clip attach the end of the paperclip to the wire coming from the buzzer.

6

Run the paperclip loop over the coathanger. What happens when you touch the coathanger?

The game

Move the paperclip loop as fast as you can along the bent wire without letting the loop touch the wire. If you touch the coathanger wire, the electrical circuit will be completed and the buzzer or lamp will operate. Time yourself and your friends. Who is the quickest? If the buzzer sounds you're out. You can make the game harder by making the paperclip loop smaller or by making the coathanger wire twistier.

Warning!
Use batteries only for your source of electricity. Never experiment with electricity from power points - it is dangerous!

Spinning color wheel

What happens when you spin a rainbow?

You will need:

a piece of white cardboard, at least 6" x 6"
red, orange, yellow, green, blue and deep purple paint
approx. 36" of string
a compass
a protractor

THE EXPERIMENT

1

Using the compass draw a circle with a 5" diameter. Make sure the point of the compass marks the cardboard so you know where the center of the circle is.

2

Cut out the circle (or you may find it easier to cut it out after Step 6).

3

Draw a line through the center of the circle.

4

Using the protractor, divide the circle into 6 equal segments.

5

Color the sections in this order: red, orange, yellow, green, blue, deep purple.

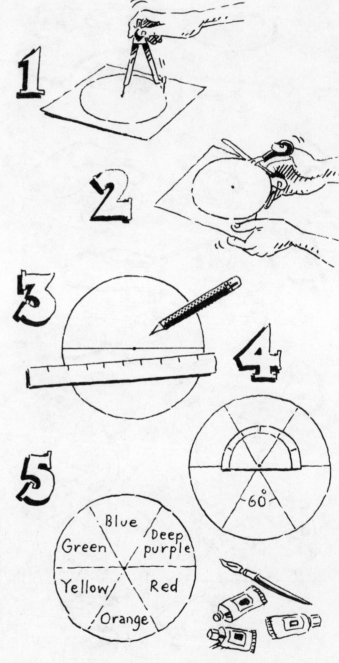

28

6
Choose one of the diameters of the circle and mark a point on either side of the center, each half an inch from the center. Make holes at each of these points.

7
Thread the string through the holes and tie the ends together.

8
Hold each end of the string and get a friend to help you rotate the disc until the string is twisted fairly tightly.

9
Firmly but gently pull the string. What do you see?

Why did the colors on the wheel change?

Ordinary light, or white light, is a mixture of the colors you used to paint the wheel. When the disc is spinning rapidly, the colors become mixed up, thus forming white. You may not be able to get a totally clear white, but see how close you can get.

Experimenting further with colors

Make a simple top with cardboard and a pencil.

Cut out as many cardboard discs as you like and mark the center of each. Paint the discs in different colors (equal sections for each color), place each over a pencil and spin it.

What color do you see when the top is spinning?

Mapping your tongue

You probably know that your tongue is covered in taste buds, but did you know there are different types of taste buds?

You will need:

5 small glasses
1 teaspoon vinegar
1 teaspoon sugar
1 teaspoon salt
1 teaspoon lemon juice
a packet of cotton buds
a sheet of paper, 8" x 10"
a pencil
a friend
dark fabric for a blindfold
water

THE EXPERIMENT

1
Half-fill four glasses with water and fill a fifth one for rinsing your mouth after each tasting.

2
Add some vinegar to the first glass, sugar to the second, salt to the third and lemon juice to the fourth. Then label each cup.

3
Draw an outline of your tongue and divide it into five areas as shown.

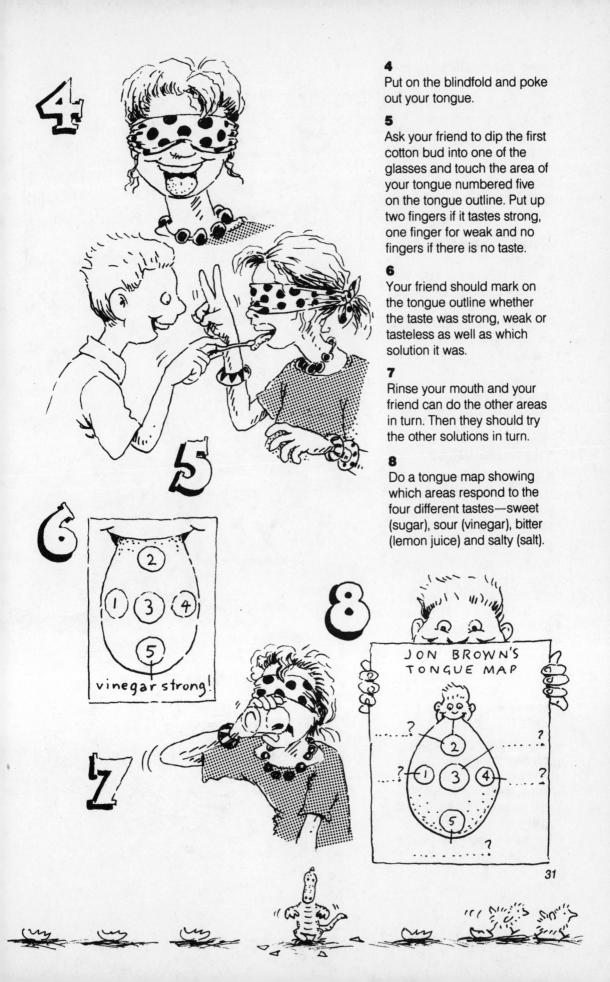

4

Put on the blindfold and poke out your tongue.

5

Ask your friend to dip the first cotton bud into one of the glasses and touch the area of your tongue numbered five on the tongue outline. Put up two fingers if it tastes strong, one finger for weak and no fingers if there is no taste.

6

Your friend should mark on the tongue outline whether the taste was strong, weak or tasteless as well as which solution it was.

7

Rinse your mouth and your friend can do the other areas in turn. Then they should try the other solutions in turn.

8

Do a tongue map showing which areas respond to the four different tastes—sweet (sugar), sour (vinegar), bitter (lemon juice) and salty (salt).

vinegar strong!

JON BROWN'S TONGUE MAP

How does your tongue taste?

Your tongue has lots of tiny taste buds for detecting different flavors. There are four different sorts of taste buds for picking up different tastes and they are found on different parts of your tongue.

Fool Your Taste Buds

Why does food seem to lose its taste when you have a head cold? This experiment shows how the senses of smell and taste work together.

You will need:

a few instant coffee granules

THE EXPERIMENT

1
Hold your nose tight, stick out your tongue and place the coffee granules on it.

2
Still holding your nose tightly, chew the coffee. Roll it around on your tongue. Can you taste it?

3
Let go of your nose. Can you taste it now?

How does your nose taste?

Taste buds on your tongue only taste certain things. Detecting some flavors, like coffee, needs the sense of smell as well. That's why food often seems tasteless when you have a head cold and your nose is congested.

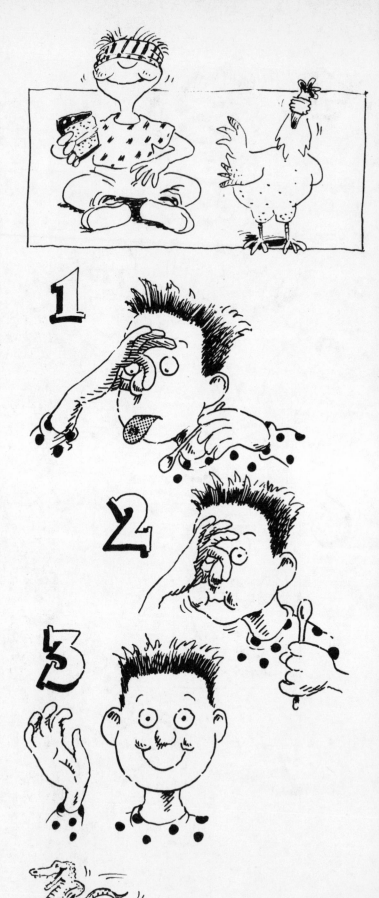